Arnold Henry Guyot

**Creation**

The Biblical Cosmogony in the Light of Modern Science

Arnold Henry Guyot

**Creation**
*The Biblical Cosmogony in the Light of Modern Science*

ISBN/EAN: 9783337253110

Printed in Europe, USA, Canada, Australia, Japan

Cover: Foto ©Lupo / pixelio.de

More available books at **www.hansebooks.com**

# CREATION

# LIST OF ILLUSTRATIONS.

PLATE
- I.—PRIMITIVE NEBULA, . . . *Frontispiece.*
- II.—CIRCULAR NEBULA — SPIRAL NEBULA,
  *To face p.* 65
- III.—THE PHOTOSPHERE OF THE EARTH DISAPPEARING, . . . *To face p.* 72
- IV.—SILURIAN AGE, . . . " 95
- V.—DEVONIAN AGE, . . " 103
- VI.—CARBONIFEROUS AGE, . . " 110
- VII.—MESOZOIC AGE, . . " 114
- VIII.—TERTIARY AGE (Dinotherium), . " 118
- IX.—TERTIARY AGE (Mammoth), . " 121

*The geological illustrations are engraved from photographs of original paintings, belonging to the series executed by B. W. Hawkins, Sc.D., for the E. M. Museum of Geology and Archæology of the College of New Jersey, Princeton.*

# CREATION

OR

## THE BIBLICAL COSMOGONY IN THE LIGHT OF MODERN SCIENCE

BY

ARNOLD GUYOT, LL.D.

BLAIR PROFESSOR OF GEOLOGY AND PHYSICAL GEOGRAPHY IN THE
COLLEGE OF NEW JERSEY. AUTHOR OF "EARTH AND
MAN." MEMBER OF THE NATIONAL ACADEMY
OF SCIENCES OF AMERICA. ASSOCIATE
MEMBER OF THE ROYAL
ACADEMY OF TURIN,
ETC., ETC.

NEW YORK
CHARLES SCRIBNER'S SONS
1884

TROW'S
PRINTING AND BOOKBINDING COMPANY
NEW YORK.

TO MY BELOVED WIFE,

WHOSE EVER READY HEART AND
HAND, THROUGH GENTLE MINISTRY DURING
LONG WEEKS OF ILLNESS, ALONE HAVE RENDERED
POSSIBLE THE ISSUE OF THIS LITTLE BOOK, THESE LEAVES
ARE OFFERED AS A TRIBUTE OF THE PROFOUND
AFFECTION OF HER ATTACHED HUSBAND

THE AUTHOR

# PREFACE.

In the beginning of the winter of 1840, having just finished writing a lecture on the Creation which was to be a part of a public course of Physical Geography that I was then delivering at Neuchatel, Switzerland, it flashed upon my mind that the outlines I had been tracing, guided by the results of scientific inquiry, then available, were precisely those of the grand history given in the First Chapter of Genesis. In the same hour I explained this remarkable coincidence to the intelligent audience which it was my privilege to address. Before that time, though acquainted with the principal attempts to put that most ancient writing in accordance with the geology of the day, I had found them entirely inadequate, and had suspended my judgment on the question—waiting for more light.

A further study of this interesting subject allowed me to perfect many a detail, and, though the general outlines remained the same, to perceive more and more the deep philosophical meaning of the plan and the connection of all the parts of that wonderful Record.

Since that time I have been requested again and again to express these views, both in private and in public, but they first appeared in print in the *Evening Post*, March, 1852, as a series of abstracts from a public course of lectures which I was delivering in New York.

The substance of these articles furnished the foundation of an extensive critical review of the same ideas, by Rev. Dr. O. Means, in the *Bibliotheca-Sacra* of March and April, 1855, in connection with other proposed explanations of the biblical account of creation.

Later still I was called upon to lecture on this subject in the College of New Jersey; and several years in succession in the Theological Seminary of Princeton. At the request of the Trustees of the Union Theological Seminary of New York, I expounded the same views in a course of twelve lectures, in the year 1866, on the Morse Foundation, then just established.

Prof. J. D. Dana did me the honor to endorse them, almost in full, in his remarkable article, on "Science and the Bible," in the January number of the *Bibliotheca-*

*Sacra*, in 1856. He also adopted them in his manual of Geology, which first appeared in 1863.

A complete though much condensed exposition was given, by invitation, before the Evangelical Alliance assembled in New York, in 1873, which is found printed in the volume of its Proceedings, New York, 1874.

These dates may serve to show that whatever be the value of this interpretation, in making clear the true meaning and import of the First Chapter of Genesis, it has been worked out independently of later publications giving the same or similar opinions.

Having been repeatedly asked by intelligent laymen, as well as clergymen, where an exposition of my views could be found, it became evident to me that, owing to the limited circulation of the Evangelical Alliance volume, the paper did not attain the full measure of its usefulness. This conviction induced me to yield to the request to publish it in a more accessible and convenient form, with such additions and illustrations as might elucidate the subject more fully.

The results of the so-called modern, higher criticism, whose object is to shake the faith in the authenticity of the Book of Genesis, have not even been alluded to. These conclusions have often been fully refuted by more competent men than their authors.

It seemed best to retain the synoptical character of the article. Experience has taught me that extended critical discussions on all the possible interpretations of the text, or on the philological meaning of certain words, are likely to engender confusion and perplexity, rather than to establish a definite and well-grounded conviction on the subject.

I have faith in the power of a simple and clear presentation of the truth. Such an one has been attempted here. May my brother scientist, as well as the believer in the Bible, find in the following pages new reasons for accepting the truths contained in this sacred document as the revelation of a God of love to man.

A. GUYOT.

PRINCETON, NEW JERSEY, December, 1883.

# CONTENTS.

### I.
INTRODUCTION, . . . . . . . 1

### II.
PLAN OF THE BIBLICAL ACCOUNT OF CREATION, . 9

### III.
WHAT THE RECORD TEACHES, . . . . 20

### IV.
WHAT HELP CAN MODERN SCIENCE GIVE US IN UNDERSTANDING ARIGHT THE STATEMENTS OF THE BIBLE, AND HOW DO THE TWO RECORDS COMPARE? . . . . . . . . 24

### V.
THE PROLOGUE, . . . . . . 29

### VI.
THE PRIMITIVE STATE OF MATTER WHEN FIRST CREATED, . . . . . . . 33

### VII.
THE FIRST COSMOGONIC DAY, . . . . 43

## CONTENTS.

### VIII.
Second Cosmogonic Day, . . . . . 54

### IX.
Third Cosmogonic Day, . . . . . 72

### X.
Third Cosmogonic Day continued, . . . . 83

### XI.
Fourth Cosmogonic Day, . . . . . 92

### XII.
Fifth Cosmogonic Day, . . . . . 95

### XIII.
Sixth Cosmogonic Day, . . . . . 120

### XIV.
Sixth Cosmogonic Day continued, . . . . 122

### XV.
The Seventh Day. The Sabbath of Creation, . 131

### XVI.
Conclusions, . . . . . . . 137

# CREATION;

OR,

## THE BIBLICAL COSMOGONY IN THE LIGHT OF MODERN SCIENCE.

---

## I.

### INTRODUCTION.

*The Biblical Narrative and the Ancient Cosmogonies contrasted—The two Records: Bible and Nature—The true Method of the Interpretation of Both—Our Point of View.*

THE sacred volume, containing the revelations that God, in his wisdom, chose to give to man, fitly opens with a short account of the creation of the material world, animated nature, and of man himself. On this great question of Creation, which implies the relation of God to his creatures, of the finite to the infinite—a question insoluble for human philosophy—man had to be taught from on high.

In all ages of history men have acknowledged the necessity of such a revelation. In the organized, primitive, as well as in the later communities, we always find as a part of the religious code of laws on which the social order is founded, a similar history of the creation of the universe—a cosmogony—for which their authors claim a divine origin.

The Bible narrative, however, by its simplicity, its chaste, positive, historical character, is in perfect contrast with the fanciful, allegorical, intricate cosmogonies of all heathen religions, whether born in the highly civilized communities of Egypt, the Orient, Greece, or Rome, or among the savage tribes which still occupy a large portion of our planet. By its sublime grandeur, by its symmetrical plan, by the profoundly philosophical disposition of its parts, and, perhaps, quite as much by its wonderful caution in the statement of facts, which leaves room for all scientific discoveries, it betrays the supreme guidance which directed the pen of the writer and kept it throughout within the limits of truth.

In all these respects this most ancient of written documents deserves special attention on the part of all enlightened minds, while the sacredness of its character doubles for us the duty of studying it in a reverent, but candid, impartial, and truth-loving spirit.

Side by side, another manifestation of the same divine mind, the book of Nature, itself the work of God, is open to our curious gaze. To man alone, among all created beings, has been granted the privilege of reading in it, by patient and intelligent researches, the innumerable proofs of the almighty power and wisdom of its author; for man's mind alone, in the world known to us, is akin to the mind which devised the wonderful plan unfolded in that great Cosmos which we call Nature.

Both these books, the Bible and Nature, are legitimate sources of knowledge; but to read them aright we must remember the object and true character of their respective teachings, which are by no means the same.

The chief design of the Bible, throughout the sacred volume, is to give us light upon the great truths needed for our spiritual life; all the rest serves only as a means to that end, and is merely incidental.

In the first chapter of Genesis, when describing in simple outlines the great phases of existence through which the universe and the earth have passed, the Bible does not intend to reveal to us the processes by which they have been brought about, and which it is the province of astronomy, chemistry, and geology to discover; but, by a few authoritative statements, to put in a strong light the relations of this finite, visible world to the spiritual, invisible world above, to God himself. Its teachings are essentially of a *spiritual, religious character.*

Destined for men of all times and of all degrees of culture, its instructions are clothed in simple, popular language, which renders them accessible alike to the unlearned, to the cultivated man, and to the devotee of science.

The knowledge we derive from Nature reaches us only by our senses. A faithful study of God's visible works, and sound deductions from the facts carefully ascertained are the foundations on which the science of nature rests. But from these finite premises no logical process can derive the great truths of the infinite, supernatural world which are given in the Biblical narrative. Nature's teachings, grand as they are, belong to the finite world, they are of a material and intellectual order, and cannot transcend their sphere. If the immensity of the boundless universe, in the midst of which we live, awakens in us the idea of the infinite, it cannot prove it, nor, governed as it is, by the necessary operation of invariable laws, can this visible world throw any light upon the mysteries of that invisible domain in which love and freedom reign supreme.

Let us not, therefore, hope, much less ask, from science the knowledge which it can never give; nor seek from the Bible the science which it does not intend to teach. Let us receive from the Bible, on trust, the fundamental truths to which human science cannot attain, and let the results of scientific inquiry serve as a running commentary to help us rightly to understand the comprehensive statements of the Biblical account which refer to God's work during the grand week of creation. Thus we shall be convinced, if I do not greatly err, that the two books, coming from the same Author, do not oppose, but complete one another, forming together the whole revelation of God to man.

In reading the Biblical narrative, to cling to an interpretation obviously disproved by the testimony of God's works, as many well-meaning, but unwise believers have done, is to refuse the light placed before us by God himself. On the other side, to decline, as many still do, *a priori*, to believe in the possibility of this antique document agreeing in its statements with modern science, because its author could not have had, it is supposed, such knowledge, before the discoveries of our day, is to be governed by a preconceived opinion. This question should be submitted to an impartial examination, as a question of fact. To do otherwise is as unscientific as it is unjust.

If we do neither, but, without prejudice, faithfully use all the means of interpretation at our disposal, we may hope to see this question of fact decided in the affirmative, and the clouds which have obscured the majestic simplicity of that noble record dispelled forever.

In offering a simple and clear exposition of his own matured views, the writer is not without strong hope that the reasons which have determined his conviction may equally satisfy the minds of his fellow-seekers after truth, whether in the domain of Nature, or in that of Holy Writ.

Taking this view of the Biblical account of creation, and of the method of its interpretation, let us consider:

The plan of the narrative.

What it teaches.

What help modern science, by its best results, can give us in understanding aright the concise statements of the Bible which relate to the method of creation.

This last investigation will tell us whether or no, and in what measure, the two records differ or agree.

## II.

#### PLAN OF THE BIBLICAL ACCOUNT OF CREATION.

The document before us for examination begins with the first chapter of the Book of Genesis and ends with the third verse of the second chapter. It is complete in itself, forming an organic whole which unfolds the history of the creation of the material universe and of living beings, including man as a part of nature.

By the symmetrical regularity of its arrangement, by the tone of its language, and the specific use of certain words, it is stamped with an individuality not to be mistaken. In this the name of God is in the plural form, *Elohim*, the triune God of the universe, the Father, the Word, and the Spirit, who all appear in the work of creation.

In the second narrative, beginning with the fourth verse of the second chapter, which takes up, under another aspect, the creation of man as the head of the family of humanity, and specifically of the Jewish people, chosen by God as its spiritual representative, guardian of the true knowledge of God and of His oracles concerning the promised Redeemer, God's name is *Jehovah*.

That difference in the name of the Creator in the two documents, the Elohistic and the Jehovistic, as they have been termed, has caused many to believe that both were not due to the pen of the same author, or that Moses had before him two ancient documents which he simply admitted in his Book of Genesis. This may, or may not be so. It is not the place to discuss this question, since we only propose to examine the first narrative *in itself*, without regard to the sources of information at the disposal of its author. We may say, however, that the obvious difference in the aim of each narrative seems sufficient to justify the difference in the expressions used in describing the creation of man and woman and in the name of the Creator, without recurring to a double authorship which is in itself improbable.

The Biblical account of creation is not an ordinary narrative. The majesty of its simple and almost rhythmic language gives it the charm of a grand poem, with a prologue, a developing drama, and a triumphant conclusion. Moreover, a closer analysis reveals a plan profoundly philosophical, which has been too much overlooked by its expositors, but will be noted here, though its full signification will be shown hereafter.

The history of Creation is given in the form of a grand cosmogonic week, with six creative or working days, preceded by an introduction, and closing with a day of rest—the Sabbath of God as a Creator.

Each day is marked by a special work, and begins with an evening followed by a morning. These six days are subdivided into two symmetrical series of three days each. Both series begin with Light—the diffused, cosmic light in the first, the concentrated solar light in the second. In both series the third day has *two* works, while the others contain but one. The first series describes the arrangement of the material world—it is the *Era of matter;* the second, the creation of organized beings, animals and man—it is the *Era of life:* two trilogies in this great drama of creation, corresponding to the two great spheres of existence which precede the historical age of man. Such symmetry of plan cannot be accidental: it is full of meaning, as we soon shall see.

The following tableau will put in a clear light the symmetrical arrangement of the parts and the special work of each cosmogonic day.

The translation of the text, here given, which adheres closely to the original, was made at my request by Prof. Henry C. Cameron, to whom I offer my sincere acknowledgment.

## THE PROLOGUE.

### a. THE PRIMORDIAL CREATION.

In the beginning God created the Heavens and the Earth.

### b. THE PRIMITIVE STATE OF MATTER.

And the Earth was desolateness and emptiness,
And darkness was upon the face of the deep,
And the Spirit of God brooded upon the face of the waters.

## ERA OF MATTER.

### FIRST COSMOGONIC DAY.

WORK.—*First Activity of Matter—Cosmic Light.*

And God said, "Let Light be," and Light was.
And God saw the Light that it was good.
And God separated the Light from the darkness.

And God called the Light Day, and the darkness
    he called Night.
And evening was, and morning was, day one.

### SECOND COSMOGONIC DAY.

WORK.—*Organization of the Heavens.*

And God said, "Let there be an Expanse in the
    midst of the waters,
And let it separate the waters from the waters."
And God made the Expanse,
And separated the waters under the Expanse from
    the waters above the Expanse.
And it was so.
And God called the Expanse Heavens.
And evening was, and morning was, day second.

### THIRD COSMOGONIC DAY.

FIRST WORK.—*a. Formation of the Earth.*

And God said, "Let the waters under the Heavens
    be gathered to one place,
And let the dry land appear."
And it was so.
And God called the dry land Earth, and the gather-
    ing of the waters called he Seas.
And God saw that it was good.

SECOND WORK.—*b. The Plants.*

And God said, "Let the earth bring forth vegetation, herb bearing seed, fruit tree yielding fruit after its kind whose seed is in it, upon the earth."

And it was so.

And the Earth brought forth vegetation, herb bearing seed after its kind, and tree yielding fruit whose seed is in it after its kind.

And God saw that it was good.

And evening was, and morning was, day third.

## ERA OF LIFE.

### FOURTH COSMOGONIC DAY.

THE WORK.—*The Solar Light.*

And God said, "Let luminaries be in the Expanse of the Heavens to separate the day from the night;

And let them be for signs, and for seasons, and for days and for years.

And let them be for luminaries in the Expanse of the Heavens to give light upon the Earth."

And it was so.

And God made the two great luminaries,

The great luminary for the dominion of the day,

The small luminary for the dominion of the night;

The stars also.

And God placed them in the Expanse of the Heavens
To give light upon the Earth,
And to rule over the day and over the night
And to separate the light from the darkness.
And God saw that it was good.
And evening was, and morning was, day fourth.


### FIFTH COSMOGONIC DAY.

THE WORK.—*Creation of the Lower Animals, in Water and Air.*

And God said, "Let the waters teem with creeping creatures (swarm with swarmers), living beings,
And let birds fly over the earth, across the face of the expanse of the heavens."
And God created the great stretched-out sea monsters (tanninim),
And all living creatures that creep, which the waters breed abundantly after their kind,
And every winged bird after its kind.
And God saw that it was good.
And God blessed them, saying,
"Be fruitful and multiply,
And fill the waters in the seas,
And let the birds multiply on the earth."
And evening was, and morning was, day fifth.

## SIXTH COSMOGONIC DAY.

**The First Work.**—*a. Creation of Higher Animals on Land.*

And God said, "Let the Earth bring forth the living creature after its kind, cattle and creeping things,
And beasts of the earth after their kind."
And it was so.
And God made the beasts of the earth after their kind,
And the cattle after their kind,
And every creeping thing of the ground after its kind.
And God saw that it was good.

**The Second Work.**—*b. Creation of Man.*

And God said, "Let us make man in our image, after our likeness,
And let them have dominion over the fish of the sea,
And over the birds of the heavens,
And over the cattle,
And over all the Earth,
And over every creeping thing that creepeth upon the Earth."

And God created man in his image,
In the image of God created he him;
Male and female created he them.
And God blessed them.
And God said to them,
"Be fruitful and multiply
And fill the earth and subdue it,
And have dominion over the fish of the sea
And over the birds of the heavens,
And over every living creature that creepeth upon the earth."
And God said, "Behold, I have given to you every herb bearing seed, which is upon the face of all the earth,
And every tree in which is the fruit of the tree yielding seed;
To you they shall be for food.
And to every living creature of the earth,
And to every bird of the heavens,
And to every thing that creepeth upon the earth in which there is life,
I have given every green herb for food."
And it was so.
And God saw all that he had made, and behold it was very good.
And evening was, and morning was, day the sixth.

### SEVENTH COSMOGONIC DAY.

*No Work.—Conclusion—The Sabbath.*

Thus the Heavens and the Earth were finished,
And all the host of them.
And on the seventh day God ended his work which he had made ;
And he rested on the seventh day from all his work which he had made.
And God blessed the seventh day and hallowed it,
For in it he rested from all his work which God had created and made.

Such is the regular plan of that opening chapter of the Holy Scriptures. Before we enter, however, into the consideration of its details, which to be well understood may require some explanation, let us see what are the great spiritual teachings which are obvious to all.

## III.

#### WHAT THE RECORD TEACHES.

The great spiritual truths emphatically taught by the narrative are: a *personal* God, calling into existence by his *free, almighty will*, manifested by his *word*, executed by his *spirit*, things which had *no being;* a Creator *distinct* from his creation; a universe, *not eternal*, but which had a beginning in time; a creation *successive*—the six days; and *progressive*—beginning with the lowest element, matter, continuing by the plant and animal life, terminating with man, made in God's image; thus marking the great steps through which God, in the course of ages, gradually realized the vast organic plan of the Cosmos we now behold in its completeness and unity, and which he declared to be *very good*.

These are the fundamental spiritual truths which have enlightened men of all ages on the true relations of God to his creation and to man. To understand them fully, to be comforted by them, requires no astronomy nor geology. To depart from them is to relapse into the cold, unintelligent fatalism of the old pantheistic religions and modern philosophies, or to fall from the upper regions of light and love infinite into the dark abysses of an unavoidable skepticism.

Accepted by man, these simple truths already form a code of religious doctrines which free him forever from the dread of the blind, irresistible forces of nature, whose worship is the foundation of all the polytheistic religions of antiquity; for he knows Nature to be not a huge, all-powerful, unconscious, unfeeling despot, but a creature of God, governed by His laws and subject to His supreme will.

Adding to these teachings those in the

second chapter, the great fact of the fall of man and the promise of a Redeemer, we have the *Primitive Gospel* the *Prot-evangelium* of the antediluvian Patriarchs, the preservation of which was the object of the election of Noah as the head of the new spiritual humanity, after the destruction, by the Deluge, of the unfaithful, and of the call of Abraham, another believer in that Primitive Gospel, whose descendants were to keep that blessed knowledge until the coming of Christ.

---

But thinking men, as well as men of science, crave still another view of this narrative; an intellectual view we may call it. They wish fully to understand the meaning of the text when it describes the physical phenomena of creation.

Are the statements relating to them a sort of parable to convey the spiritual truths just mentioned, or are they facts which correspond to those furnished by the results of scientific inquiry?

The answer to this question brings us to our third point, the treatment of which will occupy the remainder of these pages.

## IV.

WHAT HELP CAN MODERN SCIENCE GIVE US IN UNDERSTANDING ARIGHT THE STATEMENTS OF THE BIBLE, AND HOW DO THE TWO RECORDS COMPARE?

At first sight, the difficulties are not few. The holy record speaks of the light before the sun; of days with an evening and morning, before our great luminary could give a measure of time for them; of a firmament which separates the waters from the waters; of the earth with its continents and seas, preceding the sun and moon; of plants growing without the sunlight necessary to their existence. These are problems which require a solution.

Many, attempting to make the great periods of geology to correspond to the six creative days, failing to see that Moses confines the whole of palæontological geology, from the beginning of life in the Cambrian and Silurian, up to the Tertiary and Quaternary ages within the fifth and the sixth Cosmogonic days, could not, of course, find any correspondence and gave up the narrative in despair. Some have tried to obviate these difficulties by supposing a gap between the act of primordial creation and the work of the first day—a vast gulf into which they sink all the astronomy and geology of the past ages.

Others believe the narrative to be an accommodation to cosmogonic ideas current at the time it was written. Others again make it an ideal history having no connection with real facts in nature. Some have even gone so far as to conceive it to be a series of local phenomena which occurred during six days of twenty-four hours, representing phases analogous to those through which the earth has passed, thus disavowing its cosmogonic character as a history of the universe and the earth, and making of the account a pretended history of six solar days, founded upon imaginary facts of which geology has no knowledge.

As neither this pretended history nor the true one could have been witnessed by any human being, man having been created last, it is not conceivable that God should have chosen that mode of revelation rather than the true history of the creation.

Two fundamental errors, both refuted by Moses himself, as we shall hereafter see, have caused these misinterpretations. *First*, that the history of the earth begins at the second verse, discarding therefore the organization of the heavens and misapplying the work of the first and second day to the earth alone.

*Second*, making the six cosmogonic days solar days of twenty-four hours, whereas, according to the text, such days could only exist after the appearance of the sun on the fourth cosmogonic day.

We have no right to treat such a document lightly, when the holy writer declares that, "*Thus* the heavens and the earth were finished, and all the host of them" (Gen. ii. 1); and again, "*These* are the generations of the *heavens* and of the *earth*" (Gen. ii. 4), we must accept this solemn declaration, and believe that he intends to give us a veritable history of both.

Guided by this view, we shall consider the cosmogonic days as the organic phases, or the great periods of the history of the universe, and *not of the earth alone*, and look for the special work done in each, in the order indicated by Moses, viz., the primordial creation and primitive state of matter, first; Light as the beginning of the activity of matter and the organization of the heavens, next; the formation of the terrestrial globe of the earth, after, and the appearance of the sun and of organic life, with man, last.

After using faithfully all the light which the present science can shed upon each of these great topics, we may hope to be able to say with Moses: "These are the generations of the heavens and of the earth."

Let us now examine each portion of the narrative by itself, beginning with the prologue.

# V.

### THE PROLOGUE.

The *Introduction* to the work of the six days is comprised in the first and second verses, in which are recorded:

*a.* The primordial creation of the matter of the universe.

*b.* A description of the original state of matter when first created.

*a.* In the first verse we are taught that this universe had a beginning; that it was created—that is, called into existence—and that God was its creator. The central idea is *creation*. The Hebrew word is *bará*, translated by *create*. It has been doubted whether the word meant a creation, in the sense that the world was not derived from any pre-existing material, nor from the substance of God himself; but the manner in which it is here used does not seem to justify such a doubt. For whatever be the use of the word *bará* in other parts of the Bible, it is employed in this chapter in a discriminating way, which is very remarkable, and cannot but be intentional. It occurs on only three occasions, the *first* creation of matter in the first verse, the *first* introduction of life in the fifth day; and the *creation* of man in the sixth day.

Elsewhere, when only transformations are meant, as in the second and fourth days, or a continuation of the same kind of creation, as in the land animals of the fifth day, the word *asáh* (make) is used. *Bará* is thus reserved for marking the first introduction of each of the *three great spheres of existence*—the world of *matter*, the world of *life*, and the *spiritual* world, represented by man in this visible economy —all three of which, though intimately associated, are profoundly distinct in essence, and together constitute all the universe known to us.

Again, it is a significant fact that in the whole Bible where the simple form of *bará* is used it is always with reference to a work made by God, but never by man.

What have science and philosophy to say about it? Absolutely nothing. Creation out of nothing is a fact beyond their pale; it is the miracle of miracles. Both science and philosophy must start from existing premises, and *nothing* is no premise. Their universal, logical, conclusion, therefore, is that what *is* always *was*, in some form; and what is here called *creation* is but transformation, and, if so, that the Universe is God, or of God's substance.

Whether we conceive, with the Brahmin, that the material universe is an emanation from the Deity; or, with the old Egyptians, that it is itself a developing God; or, with modern materialism, that it is the sole existing substance, and the source of all the phenomena ever observed in nature and in man, pantheism and materialism are at the door, with all their internal impossibilities, and with all the contradictions they engender in the bosom of the free, moral, spiritual being, in the heart of humanity.

We have, therefore, to accept, on *trust*, the truth of creation as an ultimate fact, not to be reached by any reasoning process, but which, being accepted, makes clear to the mind and heart the relations of the universe, and of man to God. Thus Paul's declaration remains forever true: "Through *faith* we understand that the worlds were framed by the word of God."

Hence the necessity of a direct revelation of these fundamental truths, to which human wisdom could not attain in any other way, and which without the sanction of God's word were doomed to remain simple hypotheses, incapable of proof.

## VI.

### THE PRIMITIVE STATE OF MATTER WHEN FIRST CREATED.

*b.* This is described in the second verse: "And the earth was desolateness and emptiness; and darkness was upon the face of the deep; and the Spirit of God brooded upon the face of the waters."

Two words here—the *earth* and the *waters*—must be rightly interpreted before we can proceed with safety. After the majestic exordium in the first verse, embracing the whole creation, it is not without some surprise that in the second verse we find the narrative apparently confined to our little planet. But does (*erets*) the earth mean here our terrestrial globe, with its lands and seas, already individualized, separated from the rest of the universe, and the organization of which is mentioned later as the special work of the third day? I think not. The reasons for this conclusion are many.

1st. If *erets* were here the earth, we should have to consider the works of the first and second creative days as referring to the earth alone, and should be compelled to renounce the idea that the Biblical record intends to give us, as Moses declares, the generations of the heavens and of the earth—that is, a real cosmogony.

2d. In this case all that is found in it is but a *geological* history of our globe.

3d. Thus leaving out the *heavens* is at variance, not only with the declaration of Moses, but with the tenor of all the ancient cosmogonies of which that of the first chapter of Genesis may be regarded as a prototype.

4th. This would render, as we shall see, the reconciliation with the scientific facts, determined by physics and astronomy, for explaining the first and second day, very difficult, if not impossible.

5th. If the description of matter given in the second verse is meant to apply to a terraqueous globe, as some imagine, this state of things was no *real beginning*, but the result either of the destruction of a previous earth, or a medley of elements only partially combined.

All these difficulties disappear as soon as we admit that in the second verse *erets* is an equivalent for matter in general. The use of the concrete word *earth*, instead of the generic, or abstract, word *matter*, is common in most languages and was here a necessity, as such a word as matter does not exist in the Hebrew tongue. For all these reasons, we feel, therefore, justified in understanding *erets* in this early stage of the history of the universe, as meaning the primordial cosmic material out of which God's Spirit, brooding upon the waters, was going to organize, at the bidding of His Almighty Word, the universe and the earth.

The same may be said of the *waters* of the second verse. The Hebrew word *maïm* does not necessarily mean waters, but applies as well to the gaseous atmosphere; it is simply descriptive of the state of cosmic matter comprised in the word earth. These waters are the subtle, ethereal, fluid which, in the cosmogony of the ancient Egyptians, was supposed to extend beyond the boundaries of the visible universe, whose material had been drawn from that vast reservoir of all existence. The Bible itself gives us, in the Book of Job, in the Prophets, and in the Psalms, ample proofs of the familiarity of their authors with that grand conception which, being accepted by them, teaches us the true interpretation of the Genesiac account.

No more convincing example of the nature of the cosmogonic ideas which were current among the biblical writers, who no doubt derived them from Genesis, can be cited than the words of David in the 148th Psalm.

The Psalmist invites all creatures of God to praise Him; dividing them into two classes, "those of the heavens and those of the earth," and naming them in the order of their rank from the earth upward. "Praise ye the Lord from the heavens: praise ye Him, sun and moon: praise ye Him, all ye stars of light;" and, going still higher, "Praise Him, ye heavens of heavens;" and, last and highest, "ye waters that be above the heavens." These evidently are the "waters" of Genesis which precede the light, the firmament of heaven, and the earth and the seas. Reading a few lines farther, we have the proof that the Psalmist does not confound these waters above the heavens with the terrestrial waters of the seas and the atmosphere, for, calling upon the things of earth to praise the Lord, he names the dragons, and all deeps—the seas—fire, hail, vapors, and winds.

The sense of these two words being thus settled, every word of the second verse becomes clear and natural. The matter just created was gaseous; it was without form, for the property of gas is to expand indefinitely. It was void, or empty, because apparently homogeneous and invisible. It was dark, because as yet inactive, light being the result of the action of physical and chemical forces not yet awakened. It was a deep, for its expansion in space, though indefinite, was not infinite, and it had dimensions. And the Spirit of God moved upon the face (outside, and not inside, as the pantheist would have it) of that vast, inert, gaseous mass, ready to impart to it motion, and to direct all its subsequent activity, according to a plan gradually revealed by the works of the great cosmic days, the true nature of which we shall try to explain.

The central idea of the second verse is the state of matter when first created. The description applies, therefore, to the matter of the universe and not to that of the earth alone. The distorted and forced interpretations which have obscured the first part of the Mosaic account nearly all arise from the fundamental error which is here corrected. There is no gap between the first and second verses; no more than in any other part of the narrative. And we shall try to show that the Genesiac account is throughout, a consistent history of constant, regular, and uninterrupted progress, from this chaotic beginning to the creation of man.

Such is the statement of Moses as to the original condition of matter, and science does not tell a different story. Minerals, plants, animals—all bodies of nature—are compound results of processes which speak of a previous condition. By decomposing them, and undoing what has been done before, we finally arrive at the simple chemical elements which are the substratum of all bodies. The same again may be said of the three forms of matter—solid, liquid, and gaseous. The least defined—the one in which the atoms are the most free—is the gaseous. All bodies in nature can be reduced to this, the simplest of the forms of matter. Herschel, La Place, Arago, and Alexander, therefore, among astronomers; Ampère, among physicists; Becquerel and Thénard, among chemists; Cuvier and Humboldt, among geologists, all have arrived at the same conclusion, that this uncompounded, homogeneous, gaseous condition of matter must have been the beginning of the universe.

But by a second statement, Moses adds to these material elements another, entirely distinct from them, viz., the presence of God's Spirit as the source of movement in that limitless mass of matter. In no part of the narrative does God appear inactive.

Distinct in essence from his works, he calls them into existence by his will, manifested by his word, sustaining and organizing them by his supreme intelligence, and sanctioning them by his approval. The idea of God creating the universe as a perfect machine, acting automatically throughout the ages, according to laws established by himself, whose government he gives up, is entirely absent.

What does science say in regard to it?

The answer to this grave question must be postponed, for we shall be better able to discuss it when life is introduced into the world.

Meanwhile we will only remark that this view is not in the least inconsistent with the stability and the permanency of nature's physical laws; no more than when man uses gravitation, electricity, heat, etc., to obtain effects which the combination of these forces, acting according to their immutable laws, but left to themselves, would never produce.

Man cannot create the least particle of material force, or change its nature; this is God's province. But if these forces were not acting uniformly, and if we could not count upon their perfect stability, the world of human art and science would become impossible.

The complicated engine which produces such marvellous effects is not the result of the material elements of which it is composed, and the physical forces used in it, but it is the work of the mind of the engineer adapting them to his purpose.

# VII.

### THE FIRST COSMOGONIC DAY.

#### Light Appears.

"And God said, Let there be Light and Light was."

We now have a starting-point, but yet no activity, no progress. All beginnings are in darkness and silence. The era of progress opens with the first day's work. At God's command, movement begins and the first result is the production of light. This was no creation, but a simple manifestation of the activity of matter; for, according to modern physics, heat and light are but different intensities of the vibratory motions of matter.

To understand the process, let us also note that the present theory of light requires the presence of a general ethereal medium, in which matter is plunged, by which, it is penetrated, and which, by its vibration, is capable of transmitting movement to all parts of the universe.

Are matter and force one and the same, or is matter a sub-stratum and an instrument for force, as the body is for the mind?

This vexed metaphysical question is not likely ever to be solved. If we incline to the last view we may conceive that God *then* endowed inert matter with the forces which we find always associated with it— gravitation, the general quantitative force, and the specific qualitative forces and their correlatives. Under the uniform action of gravitation, which tends to unity, and from which no molecule can be screened by an interposing body, that immeasurable mass of gaseous matter contracts. In this process, latent heat is given out, atoms conglomerate into molecules; nearer approach begets continual chemical combinations on a multitude of points. In the more concentrated parts, heat is intensified and light is produced; and the result is the appearance in the dark space of heaven of a large luminous mass—the primitive, grand nebula—the prototype of those thousands of luminous clouds observed by the astronomer floating in the empty wastes within and beyond our starry heavens.

Though most of the nebulæ, viewed through the powerful telescopes of this scientific age, have been found to be clusters of distant or small stars, because far advanced in their development, the luminous gas forming the transparent body of many comets—the Zodiacal light, perhaps—and other gaseous heavenly bodies may serve to illustrate the condition of that primitive nebula.

The effect would be the same if, as some surmise, the nebula was composed of innumerable solid particles in a state of incandescence.

The words of the text would equally apply to the formation of several similar nebulæ in various parts of the heavens.

Thus " God *separated the light from the darkness* "—that is, the light of the nebula from the dark outside matter, as yet inactive, and from the empty space around. "And God called the light *day*, and the darkness he called *night*." Both words are here specific names used without reference to any period or succession of time.

The evening and the morning mark the beginning and the end of a day. At first sight, it seems that the order ought to be reversed, but it must be remembered that the beginning of that first great phase of development was the time of chaotic darkness, while the glorious morning which follows indicates the time during which the gradual illumination of that vast nebula is performed, and the change from darkness to light is effected. It was thus, in the nature of the process, that the evening actually preceded the morning, and so Moses expresses it. It is not, therefore, as some think, because of the custom of the Jews to reckon the beginning of the day from the eve preceding, but more probably the Jews derived that usage from the Genesiac account.

Each subsequent cosmogonic day has also its evening and morning, for each transformation of a phase of development into another implies a partial destruction of the preceding one, inaugurating a period of relative darkness followed by one of greater perfection.

Such was the *first* day, opening the series of works of that grand cosmogonic week; the first great period of development, under God's guidance, of that world of matter just created. A day, the duration of which was not measured by the course of the sun, which did not exist, nor by any definite length of time, but by the work accomplished in it.

"*And God saw the light that it was good.*"

The Creator thus approves his own work as suited to his further purposes.

---

Strange as it may seem to any one acquainted with God's work and his method in creation, one of the most serious obstacles, for the greatest number, in perceiving the harmony of the Biblical account with the observed facts deduced from science was, until lately, and even to this day, the question of the length of the six creative days. Are these days solar days of twenty-four hours, so called natural days, and has the whole creation been finished in an ordinary week, or are they periods of indefinite length of time?

That the general reader, not looking deep into the subject, should have been satisfied to regard the creative days as so-called natural days, is easily conceivable. It is less easy to understand that distinguished divines, and learned commentators, should have employed the greatest ingenuity in trying, often by the most extraordinary arguments, to defend the *prima facie* meaning of the text. Some have even imagined, for the purpose, a fanciful history of the earth, of which geology knows nothing. One of the most gifted and popular authors of this class goes so far as to give, as the true history, taught by the Bible, an aimless reiteration of the astronomical and geological phenomena which might have occurred, during six times twenty-four hours, in the little corner of the earth, where man was created, at the end of these six days.

It should be said, however, in justice to that class of expositors of the first chapter of Genesis, that the geological history of the earth had not then acquired the solid foundation of facts on which it now rests.

The tenacity with which the idea was held, that the six creative days could possibly be solar days, only shows the force of first impressions and transmitted habits, for its correctness is disproved in the most absolute manner by the text and the whole tenor of the Biblical record, as well as by the study of nature.

The reference in the Decalogue, to the seventh cosmogonic day as a foundation for the Sabbath of man, was another stumbling-block, as, at first sight, it suggests a complete similarity of the two Sabbaths.

This difficulty will be considered hereafter.

The Hebrew word *yom* (day) is used in this chapter in five different senses, just as we use the word *day* in common language:

1. The day, meaning light, cosmic light, without reference to time or succession.

2. The cosmogonic day, the nature of which is now to be determined.

3. The day of twenty-four hours which

begins in the fourth cosmogonic day, where it is said of the sun and moon, "Let them be for days and for seasons and for years."

4. The light part of the same day of twenty-four hours, as opposed to the night.

5. In Genesis ii., 4, in the *day* that the Lord God made the heavens and the earth, embracing the week of creation, or an indefinite period of time.

The days of twenty-four and twelve hours, which require the presence of the sun, are excluded from the first three cosmogonic days, since the sun made its appearance only on the fourth day. No reason is apparent in the text why the last two days should be of a different nature from the others, while the geological history of the creation of animals and man demonstrates that they are long, indefinite periods of time. The word day, as light opposed to darkness, in the first day, and again as used in the fifth sense, as embracing the whole creative week, has no application here. The cosmogonic day, therefore, only remains, and its special sense is to be determined by its nature.

We have seen already that each of these days is marked by a work, and each work is one of the great steps in the realization of God's plan—one of the great changes which constitute the organic phases of that history. Time is here without importance. It is given long or short as needed. As God's works are done by means and processes which we can study, that study tells us that for each of those great works of the creative days, their Author, before whom a thousand years are as one day,—has chosen to employ ages to bring them to perfection.

As in the growth of the plant we distinguish the germinating, the leafing, the flowering, and the seeding processes, as so many organic phases which might be called the days of the plant's history, without reference to the length of time allotted to each, so we have here the day of the cosmic light, the day of the heavens, the day of the earth, the day of the solar light, the day of the lower animals, and the day of the mammals and man; which are really the great phases of God's creation.

# VIII.

### SECOND COSMOGONIC DAY.

#### THE ORGANIZATION OF THE HEAVENS.

"And God said, Let there be an expanse (firmament) in the midst of the waters, and let it separate the waters from the waters; and God called the expanse Heavens. And the evening and the morning were the second day."

It is to be regretted that the English version has translated the Hebrew word *rakiah* (expanse) by the word *firmament*. This is due to the influence of the Latin Vulgate, which has *firmamentum* as the equivalent of the inexact στερέωμα of the Septuagint. This last word refers to the current Egyptian conception of a solid vault of heaven, separating the lower visible world from the upper world of subtle, invisible matter beyond. This view was held by the Greek translators, but is not warranted by the Hebrew text, and renders it unintelligible. If it were correct, how could it be said that God called that solid vault "heavens"?; and further, verse 20, that God created the birds to fly in the open "firmament" of heaven? In both cases *expanse* is evidently the fitting word.

The second cosmogonic day has been another stumbling-block to commentators. The difficulties they have created for themselves arose, as I have explained above, from depriving it of its cosmogonic character and belittling it by reducing the great phenomena there described to simple modifications of the terrestrial atmosphere. In doing so, they find no other explanation for the waters above and the waters below the heavens, than to consider the first as the clouds, the second as the seas, separated by an expanse of transparent air which is called the heavens. They forget how small a part of the earth is the total atmosphere which surrounds it as a thin pellicle. They forget that this thin covering of clouds is but a temporary and ever-changing one; and that the clouds are *in* that heaven rather than *above* it. They do not comprehend how small a heaven it is in which it is said, a few lines farther on, that the birds are flying. They forget that this is not the true heavens in which are spread the sun and moon and stars. They refuse to be taught by the Psalmist, whose clear and positive description gives, in the 148th Psalm, just quoted, the very order in which these various envelopes of our earth succeed each other, and in which the terrestrial phenomena, clouds, rains, hail, and winds, are so sharply defined as being below the heavens whence shines the sun and moon and stars; and where these last are said to be surmounted by the heavens of heavens and the waters above the heavens. All these are the successive, concentric heavens, each one surpassing the other in immensity, the idea of which was so familiar to the Egyptian and other ancient cosmogonies, and whose echoes we find so often throughout the Bible.

The organization of these heavens, together with the innumerable shining bodies which animate them, and not the narrow space between the clouds and the earth, is the worthy object of the work of the second cosmogonic day.

This grand day, so dwarfed and misunderstood, is the one in which are described the generations of the heavens, announced by Moses, which otherwise find no place in the narrative of the creative week. For on the fourth day, when the sun and moon are made to appear for the use of the life-system, viz.: the days and the years and the seasons, the word heavens is mentioned simply as the already existing space in which these bodies are placed.

We find a confirmation of this view of the second day in the nature of nearly all the ancient, oriental cosmogonies. In comparing the most important of them, we find traits of resemblance which seem to indicate that they had a common origin in earlier traditions, of which Moses' narrative is the true prototype, while the others give us only features distorted by the imagination of their authors. But all are intended to give the development of the universe of which the earth is mentioned as only a part.

The Egyptian cosmogony, the outlines of which bear the most resemblance to the Mosaic, may serve as an example.

The Egyptians conceived the whole universe as a gradually developing deity, composed of four great elements; the primitive spirit, or *Kneph;* the primitive matter, *Neith;* the primitive time, *Sevech;* and the primitive space, *Pascht;* none of which could be derived from the other, and which together constitute the one primitive god —a sort of quaternity, all the elements of which are material.  In this conception the spirit was not distinguished from matter, as it is in the modern sense of these words.

The universe to be developed was figured under the form of a great ball—the primitive egg—surrounded by the most subtle substance, the Kneph, brooding over it and preparing it for the further transformations.

In the bosom of this invisible deity, separate themselves, in the course of long ages, the coarser, material elements, out of which the visible universe is to be shaped by gradual development. The first product of the alliance of *Kneph* and *Neith*, spirit and matter, was *Phtah*, the primitive fire, under the action of which all the activity and life in that inner world were developed.

The next step was the separation of that vast material into two divinities—the vault of heaven, the firmament, *Pe;* the mass of the earth, *Anuke*, as yet unformed. Above the vault of heaven were the subtle, dark, ethereal substances of the primitive invisible deity. These were the waters above the heavens spoken of by most of the ancient cosmogonies. The masses of matter below, especially *Anuke*, were the waters under the heavens, out of which the sun and moon were next developed.

All these transformations consumed long periods of time. The duration of the first period, that of *Phtah*, or the universal light, could not be determined, say the Egyptians, because there was no sun to measure it. With the formation of the sun two new deities appear, *Sate*, or the illuminated half of the ball, and *Hator*, the dark half, deprived of the rays of the sun. After these, the gradual organization of the earth took place, the earth occupying the centre of the universe.

It is evident that all these so-called deities are no persons, but personified cosmical ideas, or individualizations of parts of nature, the relations of which are figured by genetic connections, and forming together a vast and complicated material polytheism, which finally embraces also the life-system and the animal worship so characteristic of Egypt.

Let us note here the *external* points of resemblance between this degenerate cosmogony and that of the Bible, its prototype.

In the Egyptian:

1. The original gaseous form, and the darkness of matter.
2. The successive transformations.
3. Phtah, the light, as the first step in this development.
4. The separation of the visible from the invisible universe, or, the waters below and the waters above the expanse.
5. The periods of development of indefinite length.

6. The sun, moon, and earth organized last.

But *inwardly* what profound contrasts!

The Bible knows:

1. God, the living God, the personal Creator, calling the universe into existence, instead of a mass of matter, eternal, unconscious, self-developing into a material world.

2. God distinct and above His creatures, preceding them in time and governing them by His supreme will, instead of one confounded with them and developing with them.

3. God ordering by His word and executing by His will every transformation.

4. God working according to a preconceived plan toward an aim which, when realized, is declared by Him *very good,* instead of a world growing by an automatic development.

In the heathen cosmogonies Nature's law governs; it is the law of necessity. In the Biblical cosmogony God reigns supreme. Nature is under the law of His free will and liberty.

Let us now see what science can tell us about the organization of the heavens.

The central idea of this day's work is *division* or *separation*. The vast primitive nebula of the first day breaks up into a multitude of gaseous masses, and these are concentrated into stars. Motion is everywhere. Gravitation and the chemical forces tend to concentrate matter around various centres, and thus to isolate them from each other; centrifugal force tends to disperse them. Under the laws of the forces of matter and motion—established by God himself, and acting under His guidance—these numberless bodies, of all forms and sizes, which fill the space and adorn our heavens, combine into those worlds and groups of worlds whose wonderful organization it is the province of astronomy to discover and describe.

It is premature to say that this noble science has as yet furnished us a satisfactory history of the generations of the starry heavens, and of their real structure.

But much has been done toward it. The grand conception of the structure of the heavens, proposed by Herschel, seems to adapt itself to the text. Gauging the heavens in all directions with his telescope he found regions crowded with stars, while in other parts they are few and far distant from each other. These appearances, says Herschel, can be accounted for by conceiving that all our visible heavens are but an immense cluster of self-luminous stars, of which our sun, with its retinue of planets, is but one, situated not far from the centre. The form of this vast cluster is that of a disk, whose outer boundary is the Milky Way. In this the stars seem ready to break up and assume the shape of the

branches of a spiral nebula. Beyond extends, in immeasurable distance, the dark abyss of space. In this, again, are thousands of nebulous masses, each of which may be a starry heaven like ours. Here we may fancy we recognize—in the cluster of visible stars, to which our sun, moon, and earth itself belong—the waters below the heavens, followed by the vast expanse beyond, containing the world of the nebulæ—the heavens of heavens, and the waters above the heavens, of which the Psalmist speaks.

According to Maedler all the heavenly bodies revolve around a common centre of gravity, situated in the region of the Pleiades.

Alexander, on the contrary, recognized in the great spiral nebulæ of Lord Rosse, whose composing stars are launched by centrifugal force into space, in parabolic lines, never to return by the same paths again, the very process by which the Creator dispersed these stars throughout the heavens, and thus peopled their empty spaces with these luminous bodies.

But whether we accept the views of Herschel, of Maedler, or of Alexander, concerning the structure and formation of the heavens, one fact admitted by all is the work of separation, of individualization, which must have preceded the present combination of the heavenly bodies, and is indicated as the special work of the second cosmogonic day.

But while that process of separation and dispersion is going on, the gradual concentration of each special sun leads to another kind of individualization of which our solar system offers the only example accessible to our observation, viz.: the formation of dark planets and satellites. While in the twin stars revolving round a common centre of gravity, we perceive the effect produced when the masses are nearly equal, in the nebulous stars of all grades we follow the gradual concentration from a gaseous state to a compact and well-defined body. In the genesis of our solar system, as explained by the genius of La Place and submitted by Stephen Alexander to exhaustive calculations, the result of which amounts almost to a demonstration of its truth, we see how a family of planets has been detached from a vast central body which holds them in bondage in their orbits by the power of its mass.

This last history, which immediately concerns the earth as one of the daughters of our sun, is so important in helping us to understand the phases of development undergone by our globe, that it may be well to give a short outline of the foundation on which it rests.

1. It is found that the distances of the orbits of the planets from the sun follow a nearly regular law, which is, that, starting from the orbit of Mercury and counting the place of the asteroids as one

planet, each succeeding orbit is about double the distance of the preceding one.

2. On the whole, the planets nearer the sun are smaller than the more distant ones.

3. Their density is increasing with their nearness to the sun.

4. All the planets and their satellites revolve around the sun in the same direction and nearly in the same plane as the equator of the sun itself.

5. The velocity of their revolution is diminishing with their distance from the sun.

6. The rapidity of their rotation on their axis, on the contrary, is increasing.

All these coincidences point to a common law which seems to indicate a community of origin.

To explain it La Place had not to go so far back as Herschel, to the point where matter begins to gather from the immensity of space around a nucleus forming a nebulous mass. He assumed, as his starting-point, the sun as a nebulous star with a powerful nucleus, revolving on its axis, and whose hot, gaseous atmosphere extended beyond the limit of the orbit of Neptune. Plunged in the cold abysses of heaven, in which it loses incessantly, by radiation, a part of its heat, it cools and contracts; its centrifugal force increasing rapidly at the same time. Under its action, the cool and heavier particles rush toward the equatorial parts, where, owing to the continual contraction of the main body, they are soon left behind in the shape of a ring similar to those which we observe around Saturn.

According to the laws of motion, the ring continues to move with the same velocity as the main body from which it is detached. But as the ring itself shrinks in cooling, its inner surface, receding from the sun, begins to move less rapidly, while the outside, approaching nearer the sun, moves with greater rapidity. The equilibrium being thus disturbed, the ring tends to break up, and the outside gaining upon the inside, the whole is rolled up into a single globular mass with a rotary motion in the same direction as that of the ring itself. The result is a planet revolving around the sun and rotating on its axis in the same direction as the sun and in the plane of its equator. By further contraction of the sun, the same process is repeated and new planets are formed. They decrease in size because the detached rings grow less at every step. They increase in density, because the later planets are detached when the density of the sun is increased. The larger planets have a more rapid rotation because they have been contracting during a longer period of time.

If by the further progress of astronomical science we find ourselves warranted in accepting the grand views of Herschel on the construction of the heavens, the explanation of the numerous forms of nebulæ and nebulous clusters as developed with great ingenuity by Stephen Alexander (in the *Mathematical Journal*), and the lucid exposition of our planetary and other solar systems by La Place, we might say with Moses, "These are the generations of the heavens."

## IX.

### THIRD COSMOGONIC DAY.

This day contains *two* works. *a.* The formation of the material globe. *b.* The introduction of the vegetable kingdom.

#### *a.* FORMATION OF THE EARTH.

" Let the waters under the heavens be gathered into one place, and let the dry land appear. And God called the dry land *earth;* and the gathering together of the waters called he *seas.*"

THE main idea is condensation of matter into the solid globe, its liquid covering and gaseous envelope. Here, as usual, Moses gives us the final result of the work, and not the process by which it was produced. For that we must ask Geology.

The structure of the hard mantle of rock which covers the unknown interior of the globe, and the nature of its strata, together

with their ever-increasing temperature downward, will bear witness to the eventful history of the past ages of our earth; astronomy and chemistry will carry us still higher up to the very birth of our planet.

The materials of that part of the earth-crust accessible to our investigation—from the alluvial surface sands and pebbles, through the sandstones, conglomerates, slates, and limestones, down to the crystalline bottom rocks—show themselves to be the *débris* of pre-existing rocks, rearranged at the bottom of the ocean; or due, as most of the limestones, to the secreting power of the polyps, protozoans, and most minute animals of the sea.

The temperature of the waters of this ocean was no higher than that of our tropical seas; for these rocks contain innumerable relics of marine animals similar to, though not identical with, those of the present day. Lower down, the crystalline rocks, mostly stratified—the so-called metamorphic rocks—still bear the mark of an aqueous origin, but also indicate a high degree of temperature in the waters, which explains both their crystalline character and the almost entire absence of traces of life in these early seas.

Coming from deeper sources still, but filling perpendicular fissures or chimneys, as in volcanoes, crystalline masses of porphyry, compact trap, basalt, and volcanic substances cross the regular strata up to the surface, and by their igneous nature reveal the existence of an internal temperature sufficient to keep rocks in a melted condition.

With these general facts in view, and aided by the light derived from chemistry, physics, and astronomy, we may distinguish, in the gradual formation of the physical globe, before the introduction of life, four periods:

1. The nebulous.

2. The mineral incandescent.

3. The period of the hot oceans.

4. The period of the cold oceans.

Admitting, as we do, the great probability of the genesis of the solar system having taken place, as described above, according to La Place; in the first period, the matter of the earth was a part of the hot atmosphere of the sun. In the slow process of contraction, consequent upon its cooling, the sun left it behind in the form of a gaseous ring. The ring breaks in several places, and is rolled up into a globular mass, which, in accordance with the laws of motion, rotates upon itself, and revolves around its present body nearly in the plane of its equator, and with the velocity imparted to it by the sun itself when it left it behind. The new globe, born from the old matter of the sun, now enters, as a *gaseous mass*, into the first period of its separate existence.

Loss of heat by radiation causes further

concentration. The molecules, brought nearer together and to the proper temperature for chemical action, now combine. A vast, long-continued, and ever-renewed conflagration, with an enormous development of heat and electricity, takes place, and the result is an incandescent, melted, mineral body, surrounded by a vast luminous atmosphere. The earth is a *sun;* quite similar, except in its mass, to the glowing orb from which the earth now receives its light, and which is slowly passing through a like period of incandescence. This is the second period of its history.

The cooling continues: a hard crust is formed on the surface of the melted body of the globe, and, when the temperature becomes low enough to admit of the chemical combination of hydrogen and oxygen into water, the ocean—which was before a part of the atmosphere in the shape of vapor—is deposited on the solid surface of the globe. The temperature of this first ocean must have been very high, owing to the immense weight of the atmosphere resting upon it. It has been calculated that when the deposition began, the temperature of the first waters could not have been less than 600° Fahr. This geological phase, though it is one through which a cooling globe has passed, has not, thus far, received the attention it deserves.

Let us try to see what this state of things implies, for it is important for the explanation of the fourth day.

The oceans were not only very warm, but must have been highly acidulated; for all the acids which form a large part of the thousands upon thousands of feet of rocks deposited since, must have been then in the atmosphere in a gaseous form.

These hot and acid waters, resting upon the old mineral crust, must have decomposed it, and a new series of chemical combinations have been formed, to which, perhaps, we may refer the deposition of the lowermost crystalline, Lawrentian rocks of Canada and other places, which are found at the base of the new terrestrial crust—the only one we actually know.

By these powerful chemical actions the earth was transmuted into a vast, galvanic pile, emitting constant streams of electricity, which, reaching the ethereal space at the boundary of the thick atmosphere, became luminous. According to Herschel, the photosphere of the sun may be due to a similar cause, and if we accept the most plausible explanation of the aurora borealis, it is but the last vestige of that electrical condition of our globe.

During this third period the earth was still surrounded by a photosphere of subdued brilliancy: it was a *nebulous star*.

The process of cooling goes on; the physical and chemical forces, thus far so active, subside and enter into a state of quiescence; the photosphere gradually disappears; the globe becomes an extinct body; the ocean cools down to the mild temperature of our tropical seas, and is ready for the introduction of living beings. The age of matter is over; the age of life is at hand. The fourth period was that of *the dark, extinct planet and the cool oceans.*

This fourth period, and perhaps the latter part of the third, are represented in the geological strata by the so-called azoic rocks, which are found in all continents.

At the beginning of this stage of the formation of the globe we have no reason to believe that the three great geographical elements were not still in the place assigned to each by their density; the solid land forming the central mass, a uniform ocean a general covering, and the atmosphere the last envelope. But somewhat later we have evidence of the appearance of the first land above the waters of the ocean. Extensive surfaces and low mountain chains, both in the Old and New World, belong to this age. Geology explains very plausibly the sinking of the large surfaces, now containing the oceans, and the rising between them of the continents and mountains by the gradual shrinkage of the cooling interior, forcing the hard external crust—which had become too large—to mould itself on the smaller sphere by folding into mighty wrinkles. This process could not be better described than by the words of Moses: "Let the waters be gathered into one place, and let the dry land appear"—implying that the land was already formed under the surface of the ocean, and was subsequently raised above it.

Though, during this physico-chemical history of the earth, all the forces of matter were at work, it was not with equal intensity. The most general — gravitation—prevailed in the nebulous period; in the second stage, the power of the specific chemical forces, acting by the dry process, was greatest; in the third, these forces acted more quietly by the wet process. Later, during the era of life, the mechanical forces of the waters of the oceans —tides and waves—and land waters, to which are due the formation of most of the strata composing the earth crust, became altogether prevalent. Thus every period owes its specific character to the greater activity of one of the material forces at work.

The first part of this third day closes the era of matter.

In summing up the creative work accomplished during the three cosmogonic days, we can easily recognize in this world of matter the same method of successive development as was employed by the Creator in the world of life.

Matter, a dark, uniform, inactive, gaseous fluid, is the starting-point. General activity with movement and light is the first step; breaking up into different individual bodies, scattered through the heavens, is the second; combination in organized groups, and concentration into organized individuals—as we have been able to follow it up in the formation of the sun and the earth—is the third, thus preparing the world of matter for the world of life.

But in this third day there is a second work, entirely unlike the first, belonging to the age of organic life: the creation of the plant.

# X.

## THIRD COSMOGONIC DAY CONTINUED.

### *b.* Vegetation Appears.

> "And God said, 'Let the earth bring forth vegetation, herb bearing seed, fruit tree yielding fruit after its kind, whose seed is in it upon the earth;' and it was so.
>
> "And the earth brought forth vegetation, herb yielding seed after its kind, and tree yielding fruit whose seed is in it after its kind; and God saw that it was good.
>
> "And evening was, and morning was; day third."

WITH the appearance of vegetation the history of the earth enters into an entirely new phase. It is the beginning, or the heralding of the Era of life.

When passing from the phenomena of inorganic nature, or dead matter, into those of organic nature, we find ourselves in an entirely new domain, whose laws show no similarity to those of the preceding one.

In organized beings a new, immaterial principle, superior to matter, governs the material molecules so as to make them assume new forms unknown to the mineral.

The hundred thousand forms of plants known to botanists are composed, in the main, of but few of the sixty-six chemical elements. Carbon, hydrogen, oxygen, and some nitrogen are made to combine in a limited number of complex compounds, before unknown to chemistry, and which constitute the chief substance of all vegetation.

The mode of growth in the two realms is totally unlike.

The most minute incipient crystal has the same form, the same plane surfaces with sharply defined angles, as the largest crystal of the same kind, and grows without definite limitation by the outward addition of similar figures, all parts being alike. The crystal is a fixed form. It does not die, like the plant, by an inward process, but continues to exist until it is destroyed by external causes.

The fundamental organ of both plants and animals is a flexible, globular molecule—the cell—already containing fluid in motion, and growing by inward division.

The plant is developed from a germ or living seed, growing downward in the root, and upward through successive stages in the stem, the leaf, the flower, and terminates the cycle of its individual life by the formation of a new seed, destined to reproduce its like. An ever-circulating fluid, the sap, is bringing food to all its parts.

In the plant, as in every organized being, there is an inward principle, of individuality, involved in the seed—a soul—not possessed by the crystal, with a variety of organs and functions working toward a common aim, for the benefit of the individual. An inward growth with a beginning and a definite end, and a power of reproduction which perpetuates the species; phenomena which are all absolutely foreign to inorganic matter.

Should that principle of life be removed movement ceases, the growth is stopped, the inorganic molecules recover their freedom and return to their allegiance, while the organic body decomposes, loses its form, and is destroyed. And still the chemist finds in its *débris* the identical weight and materials which were employed in its living body; none of the material molecules are lost; but the controlling power which gave them the shape of the plant is gone.

We have therefore to recognize here the introduction of a new principle. If it is not indicated in the text by *bara*, it is because it is but the peristyle of the temple of true life, the *sentient* life and the condition of its existence.

The characteristics of the plant kingdom

are admirably summed up in the words, "And God said, *Let the earth bring forth vegetation, the herb yielding seed, and the fruit-tree yielding fruit after its kind, whose seed is in itself.*"

The words "Let the earth bring forth," may seem to favor the idea of a combination of elements without the introduction of a new principle. But the same phrase is used in verse 20, when a true creation (*bará*)—that of the first animals—was meant and took place. And again, in Genesis ii., 4th and 5th, we find "in the day the Lord God made every plant of the field *before it was in the earth*, and every herb of the field *before it grew.*" This declaration distinguishes the plant life as a principle distinct from the matter which it moulds into the new form necessary for its new functions.

This view must be held as the most rational; for all experiments—even the very latest and apparently most successful—

made during the last hundred years, up to the present time, to prove the so-called spontaneous generation of organized beings from dead matter, have failed to convince the majority of thinking men of its reality. Taking into consideration the present state of our knowledge, we are obliged to admit that matter, unaided, can never rise above its own level; nor, unless associated with a new power, can it ever engender life.

The most important function of the plant in the economy of nature is, with the aid of the sun's light, to turn inorganic into organic matter, and thus prepare food for the animal. Nothing else in nature does this important work. The animal cannot do it, and starves in the midst of an abundance of the materials needed for the building up of its body. The plant stores up force which it is not called upon to use; the animal takes it ready made as food, and expends it in activity. The plant, therefore, is the indispensable basis of all animal life; for though animals partially feed upon each other, ultimately the organic matter they need must come from the plant.

The manner in which Moses introduces the creation of the plant, as a work distinct in its nature from the first work of the third day, and the position he assigns to it, within and at the end of that day, and before the creation of living beings, are highly philosophical. This order is required by the law of progress, according to which the inferior appears before the superior, because the first is the condition of the phenomenal existence of the latter.

Is this position of the plant in the order of creation confirmed by geology? If we should understand the text as meaning that the whole plant kingdom, from the lowest infusorial form to the highest dicotyledon, was created at this early day, geology would assuredly disprove it. But the author of Genesis, as we have before remarked, mentions every order of facts but once, and he does it at the time of its first introduction. Here, therefore, the whole system of plants is described in full outline, as it has been developed, from the lowest to the most perfect, in the succession of ages; for it will never again be spoken of in the remainder of the narrative.

What plants actually existed at this period geology must find out. The possibility of infusorial plants living in warm, and even in hot water, is proved by their being found in the geysers of Iceland, and in hot, acidulated springs. The latest geological investigations tell us that abundant traces of carbonaceous matter and old silicious deposits, among the so-called azoic rocks, indicate the presence of a large number of infusorial protophytes in those early seas. Whether they furnished food for the primitive protozoans of a similar grade is still a matter of doubt; but the limestone strata in the azoic age seem to speak in the affirmative.

The striking fact that Moses, though fully recognizing the great difference between the two works of the third day, and the importance of the vegetable kingdom, did not assign to it a special day, but left it in the age of matter, is not less full of meaning.

The plant is not yet life, but the bridge between matter and life—the link between the two ages. Placed within the material age of creation, it is the harbinger and promise of a more noble and better time to come. It is the root of the living tree planted in the inorganic globe, and destined to flourish in the age of life.

# XI.

### FOURTH COSMOGONIC DAY.

The fourth day opens the era of life, with the appearance of the sun, moon, and stars in the heavens visible from the earth; a work which apparently still belongs to the physical order, but whose object is to benefit life.

#### SOLAR LIGHT.

"Let luminaries be in the expanse of the Heavens, to give light upon the earth; and to separate the day from the night; and for seasons, and for days, and for years."

IF the genesis of the solar system as explained by Laplace is true, as we believe it is, the sun and moon were not then created, but they existed before, and now enter into new relations with the earth. During the age of matter, the intensity of chemical action was a source of permanent light—the earth was self-luminous, the light of the sun, moon, and stars being merged in the stronger light of its photosphere, and therefore invisible to it. But after the disappearance of its luminous envelope, our glorious heavens, with sun, moon, and stars become visible, and the earth depends upon this outside source for light and heat. Its spherical form causes the unequal distribution of both, which establishes the differences of climate from the pole to the equator. Its rotation gives, for the first time, a succession of day and night, which breaks the permanent light of the preceding ages. Its revolution round the sun brings, in their turn, the seasons and the years, Thus are prepared the physical conditions necessary to the existence of living beings, the periods of activity and rest, of summer and winter, and that variety of temperature and moisture which fosters the almost infinite richness of the organic forms of plants and animals displayed in our world of life.

In the third day the earth was ready for life; in the fourth, the heavens are ready to help in the work. The fourth day is, as it were, a reminiscence of the inorganic period, and forms another connection between the two principal stages of the globe.

Plate IV.

Radiata.   Articulata.   Mollusca.

SILURIAN AGE.

## XII.

#### FIFTH COSMOGONIC DAY.

##### CREATION OF THE LOWER ANIMALS IN THE WATER AND AIR.

"And God said, Let the waters teem with creeping creatures, (swarm with swarmers,) living beings, and let birds fly over the earth across the face of the expanse of the heavens.

"And God created the great stretched out sea monsters and all living creatures that creep, which the waters breed abundantly after their kind, and every winged bird after its kind, and God saw that it was good.

"And God blessed them, saying, Be fruitful and multiply and fill the waters in the seas, and let the birds multiply on the earth. And evening was, and morning was, day fifth."

THE fifth and sixth days offer no difficulties, for they unfold the successive creation of the various tribes of animals which people the water, the air, and the land, in the precise order indicated by geology.

This history is introduced by the solemn word *bará*, which occurs here for the second time, and gives us to understand that, with the creation of the animal, another great and entirely new order of existence begins.

All that we said on the occasion of the introduction of vegetation, as the lower realm of organized nature, applies with double force to the animal. The plant, indeed, as we have remarked, was but a preparation for the appearance of the living organized being. The variety of animal forms is many times greater. The principle of individuality becomes more intense in the animal, the variety of organs and of organic functions is greatly increased.

Matter is in the animal, but controlled and shaped into new forms foreign to its own nature, to suit the wants of the immaterial being within. Vegetative life is in it, but subservient to higher functions, which the plant could never perform by itself. A conscious perception of the outer world by *sensation*, however, and a *will* to react upon it, are powers which place the animal on a higher platform, and make it a being which, by its nature and its functions, is entirely distinct from the lower grades of existence.

Here the important question which we have already asked, again recurs: Do all these phenomena of life, so different from the simple work of the inorganic particles of matter, take place without the help of a new power, of an immaterial nature, for which matter is but an instrument for performing these higher functions; or are they merely the result of a new combination of the chemical elements, left to themselves? In other words: Can life proceed from non-living matter; or is it true that life can be evolved only from the living? All the more recent, careful experiments have demonstrated that the first is but an illusion; life alone begets life; and such reliable observers as Pasteur, Tyndall, and others, have declared the spontaneous generation an untenable hypothesis. Even the most pronounced materialists, such as Haeckel, avow that science has not yet been able to evolve life out of dead matter; but, as the latter savant naïvely expresses himself, "it must be so, for otherwise we should have to admit a miracle," which for him is an absurdity. And still this miracle did occur, for the introduction of a new element is a creation—that is, a miracle —and so the Bible says.

Let us cast a glance at the geological history of the life system, such as present science enables us to read it, and the admirable correctness of the Mosaic account will be evident.

### GEOLOGICAL HISTORY OF LIFE.

Geology informs us that the terrestrial crust, down to its lowest attainable depths, is composed of layers placed upon each other, different in mineralogical character and structure, and evidently deposited at the bottom of the ocean. The order of their superposition furnishes a sure chronological table of the events which took place during their formation; the lowermost stratum, the first deposited, being the oldest; the surface layers, the last formed, being the most recent.

These strata preserve in their folds the archives of the creation of organized beings, living at the time of their deposition, whose innumerable remains fill their rocky shelves and reveal to the geologist the order of appearance of the various tribes of plants and animals, thus enabling him to reconstruct the history of the life system, through all its gradual changes, from its earliest beginning to the present time.

Five great ages of life may be distinguished, each of them characterized by the predominance of a certain class of animals, and marking the great steps of gradual progress in the vast system of the living forms of the past.

These are preceded, as a preface, by an age of protophytes and protozoans, as yet rather vaguely determined, in the so-called azoic or archæan rocks.

1. The age of invertebrated animals, contained in the Silurian series of rocks.

2. The age of fishes, in the Devonian series.

3. The age of the first land plants, in the Carboniferous rocks.

4. The age of the reptiles, in the Mesozoic rocks—triassic, jurassic, and cretaceous.

5. The age of the mammals, in the Tertiary rocks, which is closed by the age of man, in the Quaternary or present age.

*The Age of Protophytes and Protozoans.*

The lowermost strata to which we have access are the so-called Laurentian of Canada, and analogous formations in other continents. These rocks of great thickness show absolutely no traces of life and can really be considered as the end of the azoic age of the globe. But just above them the middle Laurentians contain carbon, in the shape of graphite, and masses of limestone, both of which indicate the first signs of vegetable and animal life. It is well known that carbon, when found chemically isolated, denotes a vegetable process. A vast quantity of graphite and carbonaceous matter, found disseminated in the most ancient layers, up to the Cambrian, seems to prove the presence in the waters of a great number of protophytes whose delicate forms could not be preserved, while the solid substance — the carbon — testifies to their former existence.

The intercalated limestones, carefully examined under the microscope by Dr. Dawson, appeared to him to be fossil species of monstrous protozoans, though other skilful investigators have since refused to recognize an animal in the Eozoon Canadense. It must be confessed that this would be a natural beginning of the life system, all the more that the limestone deposits are, to a great extent, in later ages, the result of the life operations of most minute beings.

### The Cambrian and Silurian Age—Primordial Fauna.

If there is still some doubt as to the existence of life at this early stage, there is none in regard to it at the beginning of the Cambrian and the Silurian age. Here we find ourselves at once in the presence, not of doubtful animal forms, but of a complete fauna, representing the three great archetypes of invertebrated animals, the radiates, mollusks, and the articulates, with all their various subdivisions. They do not appear successively, as might be expected, in the order of their perfection, but all simultaneously, on the same

Plate V.

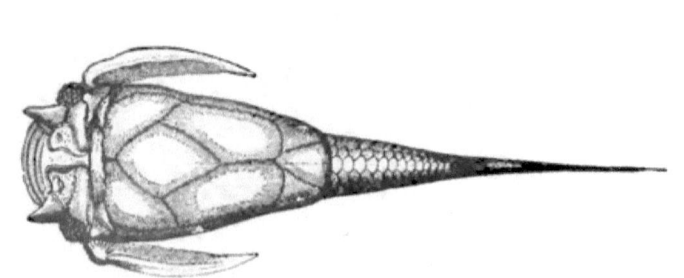

Pterichthys Cornutus.

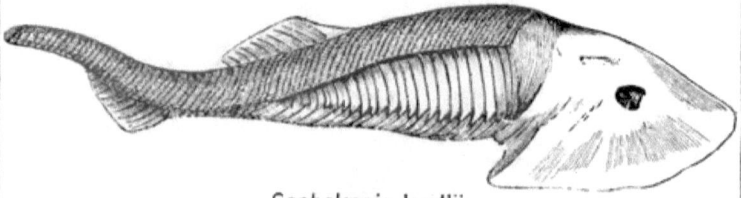

Cephalaspis Lyellii.

Dipterus.

DEVONIAN AGE—FISHES.

level, the mollusks preserving a decided pre-eminence.

During untold ages, represented by successive deposits of rocks, amounting to over twenty thousand feet in thickness, corals and plant-like radiates, mollusks of all grades—some of gigantic size—numberless crustaceans of embryonic forms, swarm in the tepid waters of the ocean; but no fishes are found, save a few at the very end of this long period, as forerunners of the higher forms which are coming. This is the reign of the lower animal life—the involuntary or instinct life—typified by the invertebrates.

### Devonian Age.

The Devonian strata contain an abundance of remains of the fish tribe, which is added to the riches of the sea, and takes the lead among the tenants of the ocean; for, though the lowest grade in the archetype of vertebrates, it belongs to the higher level of animal life, with brain, in which the sensation and will predominate. The strange forms of these first fishes, their reptilian character, their powerful organization, make them the scavengers and the kings of the seas. This is the reign of fishes.

These two long ages, the Silurian and the Devonian, were the aquatic age of the world. The whole life system was confined to the waters of the ocean. The temperature of these waters and the physical circumstances which characterized them must have been similar in all continents, for the Silurian and Devonian animals show a remarkable resemblance of species in the most widely separated regions of the globe. Though the specific forms are numerous, they are not so deeply marked.

The same aquatic character is also observed in the vegetation. The few plants which have resisted the decomposition are those which live only in the water, and nearly all belong, like the algæ, to the flowerless thallogens, whose tissues are composed exclusively of vegetable cells. In the Devonian, plants of a higher grade, belonging to the vascular cryptogams, such as the ferns, are added, and already proclaim the presence of land. But the triumphal development of vegetation takes place in the following—the Carboniferous —age, in which the superabundance of plant life becomes the chief characteristic.

### *Carboniferous Age.*

During the Devonian age, the great predominance of the sandstone formations indicated the shallowness of the seas in which these materials of the decomposing rocks, tossed about by the waves, were deposited.

In the Carboniferous age the continents, which were slowly growing under the water, reach the surface. These vast expanses of newly emerged, still swampy, lands cover themselves with a mantle of verdure. In the warm and moist atmosphere, overcharged with carbonic acid gas, humble cryptogams attain to the size of stately forest trees, and luxuriant ferns and kindred plants provide the material for the vast beds of coal so precious to civilized man. This is also an age of slow oscillations of the land. The swamp, in which were decomposed the plants which form a bed of coal, was slowly submerged and the growth of the forest stopped. New deposits of mud and sand covered that mass of vegetation, under which it was transformed into coal. A subsequent movement raised the land again above the water, the vegetative process begins anew and provides materials for another forest and another bed of coal. This process is repeated so often that we find a series of over forty similar superposed beds of coal, in the United States; sixty, in Nova Scotia, and nearly one hundred, in

England. When we reflect that it has been calculated that a luxuriant forest, like that of the valley of the Amazon, put under water, would produce only half an inch of coal, we can form an idea of the length of a geological period, implying the successive growth and transformation into coal of hundreds of forests, adorning the ground one after another, and leaving behind them beds of coal of four, eight, and twenty feet in thickness.

The Carboniferous age was pre-eminently an age of verdure. Though similar coal beds are found in every age, geology fails to record, before or after this remarkable period, a time at which these deposits are at once so extensive, so universal, and quantitatively so abundant.

But in that immense mass of vegetation, none of the present flowers, with vivid colors, enlivened the landscape. Seven-eighths of the species represented were ferns, either in the form of luxuriant foliage or in the shape of trees. The other trees, like the stately lepidodendron, are gigantic forms of the puny ground pine of the present day. The stout sigillarias with their enormous roots, the slender calamites, resembling the cane-brakes, were the principal ornaments of these dark, moist forests. All these belong, like the ferns, to the great vascular cryptogams, or intermediate forms. The only flowering trees were a small number of gymnosperms, or of the pine tribe, whose inconspicuous flowers do not modify the character of the forests but which herald a higher type of vegetation to come.

We see here, therefore, the first grand display of a land vegetation, the form of which, however, is limited to the class of plants whose botanical character is the predominance of foliage over every other part of the plant.

This age of verdure extended over the whole world; for we find it with similar characteristics, nay, similar specific form,

## FIFTH COSMOGONIC DAY.

in all the continents, though there is nowhere so great a development as in North America. Coal is found with the same species of plants from the Arctic regions, in Spitzberg, through the temperate and tropical zones, to South America, Africa, and Australia. Every one is aware of the vast importance of these enormous deposits of coal for human industry, upon which depends so much of the riches of all civilized nations.

But the coal era performed also an important function in favor of the life system, in purifying the atmosphere of its excess of carbonic acid gas. By the decomposition of that gas by the living plants, under the action of the sun, the carbon was fixed in the coal beds, while the oxygen was returned to the atmosphere, for the furtherance of animal life. The beneficial influence of this process is shown by the fact that the first air-breathing animals, such as insects and amphibians, begin to appear only in and toward the end of that period.

The progress of the life system in the Carboniferous age is not so well marked. A few small amphibious reptiles, and toward the end large types, of a mixed character already announce that the great reptilian age is at hand.

The three preceding ages together make the Palæozoic Era, or the ancient history of the life system; for it can be fitly called the time of the three great beginnings:

1. The vegetative life of the invertebrates in the Silurian.

2. The higher life of the brain animals as represented by the fishes.

3. The Carboniferous, with the first display of land life.

Now opens

### *The Mesozoic Age.*

In the Triassic, of this age, the sandstone formation, indicating a considerable

Plate VI.

B. W. Hawkins, pinx.

Lepidodendron. Sigillaria. Calamites.

CARBONIFEROUS AGE.

## FIFTH COSMOGONIC DAY. 111

destruction and reconstruction, with a meagre supply of fossils, predominates.

In the Jurassic and Cretaceous, the great abundance of limestone formations denotes a prevalence of lower marine life; the very rocks are formed by an accumulation of microscopic protozoans. The development of the invertebrates, and particularly of the mollusks, attains here its highest pitch, in the number and beauty of its most perfect form, the cephalopods. Ammonites, remarkable for their great size and their elaborate elegance and variety, and innumerable Belemnites, fill the Jurassic and the Cretaceous seas with a profusion of molluscan life which is never found again, to that degree, in later periods.

This is again the time of the formation and growth of coral reefs and coral islands, which were so well defined, that the geologists of the Jura gave a full account of their structure, before Dana and Darwin described the same phenomena as observed by them, among the thousand islands which stud the Pacific.

But by far the most important feature of this age, is the preponderance and variety of reptilian life.

Gigantic amphibians, in the first period, present a curious mixture of the characters of that class intermingled with those of the true reptiles.

The Jurassic seas were peopled with the long-necked Plesiosaurs and the stoutbuilt Ichthyosaurs, from twenty to thirty feet long.

In the great central sea, which was then covering the plains of Kansas, swam a variety of reptiles, some of which, of serpentine forms, like the Elasmosaurus and the Edestosaurus, attained the size of sixty to eighty feet and more; while the Atlantic coast was tenanted by numerous species of massive Mosasaurs.

Land reptiles were equally abundant

and notable in size. Besides the crocodile and the lizard-like Iguanodon, the Megalosaur and many others, the family of the Dinosaurs deserves a special mention. Their bird-like affinities of structure, the disproportion of their anterior legs to their hind limbs, whose length and strength allowed them to take an upright position which gave them a kangaroo-like appearance, make them one of the most remarkable families of this age of reptiles.

This family contained also the largest types of land animals that have ever existed. The Hadrosaurus of New Jersey stood erect, from twenty to twenty-five feet high. The Atlantosaurus of Colorado reached the height of from sixty to eighty feet, so that it would be difficult to understand how the strength of its muscles could have supported the weight of its bones, if it was not that the latter had been found hollow, like those of the birds.

The atmosphere also was replete with reptilian life. There were bat-like animals with enormous heads and membranous wings—the Pterodactyls—of all dimensions, from our ordinary bats to monstrous species whose expanded wings measured twenty-five feet from tip to tip. Contemporaneously with them, a wonderful family of birds, with teeth and reptilian characters, prepared the transition to the true birds, which made their appearance, in small numbers, at a later time.

A last feature of the Mesozoic age must be noted. The forest trees of the Triassic and Jurassic periods were essentially made up of Calamites, colossal Horsetails, and a majority of Gymnosperms; that is Pines, Cycads, and other Conifers.

With the Cretaceous period, the character of the vegetation changes. The classes of the Monocotyledons and the Dicotyledons show themselves in profusion. The oak, the maple, the sassafras, etc.,

Plate VII.

*B. W. Hawkins, pinx.*

Laelaps. Mososaurus. Hadrosaurus. Elasmosaurus. Pterodactylus.

**MESOZOIC AGE.**

which constitute the bulk of our present forests, are found in abundance in the temperate regions, and palm trees in the warmer latitudes. The scenery assumes altogether the modern aspect which it still retains.

No two ages in the history of the life system present a more striking contrast than this age of the mastery of reptiles, and the Neozoic, or Tertiary, which follows. These huge reptiles, which filled the water, the land, and the atmosphere, suddenly disappear after the Cretaceous. While the vegetation of the landscape remains very much the same, a new class of animals, the mammals, the typical and the highest of the vertebrates, at once take their place on the globe. During the three periods which succeed each other in that age—the Eocene, the Miocene, and the Pliocene—the various types are gradually developed; in the Eocene, mostly mixed types, which are afterwards specialized; in the Miocene, the great pachyderms, the Mammoth and the closely allied Mastodon, the group of the Herbivores, and Frugivores, including the monkeys; in the Pliocene, are added a large number of Carnivorous animals, which become characteristic of this period.

Last of all man appears, uniting in himself all the perfections of the animal kingdom, and with him a higher plane of life, which begins the moral world.

These facts speak a strong language. They tell us that *creation* is a *reality*. Besides the primordial creation of matter, that few will deny, the creation of life must be acknowledged, since, as we have seen, science has thus far been unable to derive it from dead matter by any process whatever. Scientific inquiries are far from having demonstrated that all the archetypes of the invertebrates which appear simultaneously in the Silurian, are derived from one another. Science fails to discover traces of a direct descent of the vertebrate from the invertebrate, whose plan of structure is entirely unlike; of the large fishes of the Devonian from any preceding animal form; of the huge reptiles of the middle ages of life from the fishes of the Devonian. It cannot be proved that the great pachyderms, which suddenly come upon the stage in the tertiary epoch, are the offspring of the reptiles of the preceding age. The bond which unites them is of an immaterial nature; the marvellous unity of plan which we observe is in the mind of the Creator. We should then acknowledge a *plan*, admirable in conception, perfect in execution. There is a *wisdom* which devises, a *free will*, and a *power* which executes and creates in succession, at the appointed time, when it is fitting, and not a single great unconscious whole developing by itself.

To say more for the present is to go beyond the facts as we know them. Whether the further progress of embryology will force us to modify these views remains for the future to say.

In the order of time there is progress. The inferior being always precedes the superior; the imperfect the perfect. Inorganic nature precedes organization. The watery element reigns before the terrestrial; the aquatic and inferior animals before the terrestrial and superior. In the series of the vertebrated animals, we see fishes, reptiles, birds, and mammifers appearing in the ages of the globe in the order of their perfection.

Whether or not we view this order as the result of evolution, God's guiding hand must be discerned, without which nature alone could not have produced it.

The accordance of these facts of geology with the Mosaic account is so evident that no further explanation is necessary.

It is, perhaps, here the place to note

Plate VIII.

B. W. Hawkins, pinx.
Megalosaurus. Tapirus. Palæotherium. Dinotherium.

TERTIARY AGE.

the wonderful accuracy with which Moses gives, in a few words, the characteristics of the groups of animals which he mentions. It would be difficult better to designate than as "swarmers, living beings," the prodigious quantity of small medusæ and marine animalculæ which are every day produced and swallowed by the millions, as the food of the monstrous whales. And again, no name could be better applied to the great reptiles of the Mesozoic age that he describes, than the word *tanninim*, or great stretched out sea monsters, by which they are indicated in the text.

In the Tertiary the herbivorous animals, domesticated by man, are named cattle; while the others, including the carnivorous, are called the wild beasts, and the smaller ones, the creeping things.

## XIII.

### SIXTH COSMOGONIC DAY.

The sixth day, which is the third of the era of life, contains *two* works, as did the third day of the era of matter: *a*. The creation of the higher animals, especially those living on the dry land, corresponding with the Tertiary age. *b*. The creation of man in the Quaternary age.

#### *a*. HIGHER ANIMALS. MAMMALIA.

"And God made the beasts of the earth after their kind, and the cattle after their kind, and every creeping thing of the ground after its kind, and God saw that it was good."

For this creation the word *made* is used instead of *create*, for it is not the first introduction, but the continuation of the life system.

The creeping animals of the sixth day are not reptiles, but, according to Gesen-

Plate IX.

Machairodus.   Mammoth.   Hyæna.

B. W. Hawkins, pinx.

TERTIARY AGE.

ius the smaller mammalia—rats, mice, etc.

The greatest changes in the mineral and organic creation, according to geology, took place between the cretaceous and tertiary epochs. And there, also, Moses places the beginning of a new day. For not only are the land animals a new set of beings, they are also the highest, and the family to which man belongs as a member of the life system of nature.

# XIV.

## SIXTH COSMOGONIC DAY CONTINUED.

### *b.* CREATION OF MAN.

> "And God created man in his image, in the image of God created he him, male and female created he them."

THE second work of the sixth day is of a vastly different nature from the first.

The animal kingdom, as such and in itself, is finished; but between this plane and the new sphere which is coming a link is necessary, and this link to a more exalted grade of life is man.

The creation of man is a fact of such great importance that it could not be mentioned otherwise than separately. Here again, and for the third time, the word *bará* announces, not a simple continuation of the animal, but the creation of still another order of existence, the most exalted of all. Three times, as if to emphasize the event, the potent word is repeated.

Man, made by the Creator in his own image, and upon whose creation Moses puts so much stress, to enforce, as it were, the idea of his dignity, could not be confounded with the animals. With his advent a still higher plane is introduced which comprises not only animal but spiritual life, which has its own laws, its own character, and for which the body is but an instrument—an instrument that in its service is called upon to perform much higher functions than the simple physiological ones.

That spiritual element, which constitutes man as a distinct creation, can no more be derived from the physiological functions of the animal than life can be evolved from dead matter. There is between the two planes an impassable abyss. The invisible world, the world of ideas, which contains the roots of all existence, is absolutely shut up from the animal, for he has no power to perceive it. All his knowledge comes to him through his bodily senses, which are confined to the use of his bodily wants, and, directed and limited by instinct, do not extend in any way to the region of the unseen. The animal, therefore, incapable of knowing God, is not a responsible moral agent. He is still under the law of nature, that is of instinct or necessity, while man, possessed of a knowledge of God, is under the law of liberty and thus becomes a responsible, or in other words, a moral being.

We often hear of palæontologists looking sedulously for the missing link between man and the animal. They forget that in the sense of which they speak, there can be no link wanting. The figure and the structure of the ape is as near as need be, to be called a link between man and the animal; the difference between the two beings is not in the shape of a thumb or of any particular bodily organ, but in the moral nature. An animal, as beautiful in form as Apollo Belvidere, but not possessed of the sense of the invisible, would still be an animal and nothing more. A poor misshapen Hottentot, endowed with these spiritual faculties, rendering him capable of becoming a living member of the spiritual world, through faith in Christ, would still be a man, belonging to that upper plane of life, and bound to his Maker by ties of love and adoration.

The invisible world of ideas is the true domain of man, the scene of his activity. For this reason, language has been vouchsafed to him, while it is denied to the animal, whose functions are limited to the procuring of food, to self-defense and to reproduction. Even the powers of the monkey are thus restricted. Hence the unlimited capacity for progress in man, and the completely stationary condition in the monkey tribe and in all animals, are easily explained. Nature has separated the two orders by immutable laws.

Any length of time that Darwin might desire for his transformations, would never suffice to make of the monkey a civilizable man.

The new element, therefore, which is infused into man, at his creation, is the religious element, or the capacity of being associated, in God's service, with God's life and God's perfections.

But why does Moses place this creation, not in a separate day, but with the mammalia in the sixth day?

Man is the crowning act of the Creator. He is the summary of all the perfections scattered through the animal kingdom, of which he is the head. He is the end and aim of the whole development of our planet, and as such belongs to our physical earth.

But he is also a being of a new and superior order, and therefore must be kept distinct. The appearance of the physical man is the prophecy and the promise of a future and more perfect age of development which begins with him—the age of moral freedom and responsibility—that of the historical world.

This second work of the sixth day is thus the link between the age of the physical creation and that of the moral development of mankind, as the plant was the link between the material world and that of life. It is the moral world planted in the material world, in order to make the latter subservient to a higher and better aim.

Before we leave this grand history of the creation let us offer a few remarks on the relation that it holds to evolution, the favorite doctrine of the day.

Though the narrative is, on the whole, singularly non-committal, in regard to any specific scientific doctrine, there are a few points on which it is positive. It teaches that:

1. The primordial creation of matter, the creation of the system of life, and the creation of man, are three distinct creations.

2. They are not simultaneous but successive.

3. God's action in the creation is constant.

As we have already observed, each of these great orders of things is introduced by the word *bará*, so that Moses seemed to distinguish the three great groups of phenomena as distinct in essence. According to this, the evolution from one of these orders into the other—from matter into life, from animal life into the spiritual life of man—is impossible.

The question of evolution within each of these great systems—of matter into various forms of matter, of life into the various forms of life, and of mankind into all its varieties—remains still open.

The relation of these three worlds is no less remarkable. Matter—the lowest order—is a general substratum for all the others. Aided and fashioned by the principle of life it performs higher functions in the plant and animal. Matter, plant life, and animal life perform higher intellectual and moral functions, under the guidance of the human soul.

Every one of the lower powers, associated with a higher element, becomes instrumental; the higher as a cause, the lower as a condition of existence, or as an instrument, both co-operating to a common progress.

But after each of these factors has performed its part, something yet remains to be explained. The result, varied as it may be, is never arbitrary confusion, but order and beauty; and this shows the constant and indispensable supervision of God over his work.

Here end the working days of the Creator. All his other works God had declared to be *good;* but on the sixth day "*God saw every thing that he had made, and, behold, it was very good.*"

The work of the whole week is now finished, and perfect as God will have it for his purpose—his own glory and the education of man.

## XV.

#### THE SEVENTH DAY. THE SABBATH OF CREATION.

"Thus the heavens were finished, and the earth, and all the host of them.

And on the seventh day God ended his work which he had made and rested on the seventh day from all the work which he had made.

And God blessed the seventh day and hallowed it, for in it he rested from all his work which God had created and made."

Now begins the seventh day, the day of rest, or the *Sabbath* of the earth, when the globe and its inhabitants are completed.

Since the beginning of this day no new creation has taken place. God rests as the Creator of the visible universe. The forces of nature are in that admirable equilibrium which we now behold, and which is necessary to our existence. No more mountains or continents are formed, no new species of plants or animals are created. Nature goes on steadily in its wonted path. All movement, all progress has passed into the realm of mankind, which is now accomplishing its task.

The seventh day is, then, the present age of our globe; the age in which we live, and which was prepared for the development of mankind. The narrative of Moses seems to indicate this fact; for at the end of each of the six working days of creation we find an *evening*. But the morning of the seventh is not followed by any *evening*. The day is still open. When the evening shall come the last hour of humanity will strike.

This view of the Sabbath of creation has been objected to, on account of the form of the command in the Decalogue, relating to the observance of the Sabbath. But those who object, confound God's Sabbath with man's Sabbath, and forget the words of Christ, that our Sabbath was made for man, who needs it, and not for God. God rests as a Creator of the material world only to become active, nay, Creator in the spiritual world. His Sabbath work is one of love to man—the redemption. His creation is that of the new man, born anew of the Spirit, in the heart of the natural man. So man is commanded to imitate God in leaving once in seven days the work of this material world, to turn all his attention and devote his powers to the things of heaven.

There are, therefore, *three* Sabbaths:

1. God's Sabbath, after the material creation.

2. The Sabbath of humanity, the promised millennium, after the toil and struggle of the six working days of history.

3. The Sabbath of the individual, short-lived man, the day of rest of twenty-four hours, made for him according to his measure.

The length of the day in each, is of no account. The plan, in all, is the same, and contains the same idea—six days of work and struggle in the material world, followed by a day of peace, of rest from the daily toil, and of activity in the higher world of the spirit. For the Sabbath is not only a day of rest, it is the day of the Lord.

The following tableau, summing up the results of the preceding discussion, may be found of service in making clear the correspondence between the record of Moses and that of science.

Whatever be the opinion which we may entertain as to the correctness of the history of the creation of the universe and the earth, such as the present results of inductive science can furnish, we may affirm that the best explanation science is now able to give, on this great topic, is also that which best explains, in all its details, the first chapter of Genesis, and does it justice.

# XVI.

### CONCLUSIONS.

Such is the grand cosmogonic week described by Moses. To a sincere and unprejudiced mind it must be evident that these great outlines are the same as those which modern science enables us to trace, however imperfect and unsettled the data afforded by scientific researches may appear on many points.

Whatever modifications in our present view of the development of the universe and the globe may be expected from new discoveries, the prominent features of this vast picture will remain, and these only are delineated in this admirable account of Genesis.

These outlines were sufficient for the

moral purposes of the book; the scientific details are for us patiently to investigate. They were, no doubt, unknown to Moses; as the details of the life and of the work of the Saviour were unknown to the great prophets, who announced his coming and traced out with master hand his character and mission, centuries before his appearance on the earth.

But the same divine hand which lifted, for Daniel and Isaiah, the veil which covered the tableau of the time to come, unveiled to the eyes of the author of Genesis, by a series of graphic visions and pictures, the earliest ages of the creation. Thus Moses was the prophet of the past, as Daniel and Isaiah and many others were the prophets of the future.

THE END.

# ERA OF MATTER.
*Introduction.*

| THE BIBLE. | SCIENCE. |
|---|---|
| In the beginning God created the Heavens and the Earth. And the Earth was desolateness and emptiness; and darkness was upon the face of the deep. | Matter is not self-existent. Primitive state of matter. Gas indefinitely diffused. |
| *First Day.* And God said, Let Light be, and Light was. And God separated the light from the darkness. | *First Activity of Matter.* Gravity. Chemical Action. Concentration of diffused matter into one or more *nebulæ*, appearing as *luminous* spots in the *dark* space of heaven. |
| *Second Day.* And God said, Let there be an expanse in the midst of the waters. And God made the expanse, and separated the waters under the expanse from the waters above the expanse. | *Division.* The primitive nebula is divided into smaller nebulous masses. Formation of the visible, lower, starry world. |
| *Third Day.* a. And God said, Let the water under the Heavens be gathered to one place and let the dry land appear. b. And God said, Let the earth bring forth vegetation. | *Concentration.* The nebulous masses concentrate into stars. Our sun becomes a nebulous star. Formation of the mineral mass of the earth by chemical combination of the solid crust, the ocean, and atmosphere. The earth self-luminous; a sun. First appearance of land. Azoic rocks. First infusorial plants and protophytes. |

## ERA OF LIFE.

*Fourth Day.*
And God said, Let luminaries be in the expanse of the Heavens to separate the day from the night, and they shall be for signs, and for seasons, and for days, and for years.

Chemical actions subside. The earth loses its photosphere; sun and moon become visible. First succession of day and night, of seasons and years. Differences of climate begin. Archæan rocks. Protophytes. Protozoans.

*Fifth Day.*
And God created the great stretched out sea monsters and all living creatures that creep, which the waters breed abundantly, and every winged bird.

Plants and animals appear successively in the order of their rank — marine animals, fishes, reptiles, and birds. First great display of land plants. Coal beds. Paleozoic and Mesozoic ages.

*Sixth Day.*
a. And God made the beasts of the earth, and the cattle and every creeping thing of the ground after its kind.
b. And God created man in his image.

Predominance of mammals; the highest animals. The beasts of the earth. Carnivorous; the cattle, Herbivorous animals. Tertiary age. Creation of man. Quaternary age.

*Seventh Day. — Sabbath.*
And God saw all that he had made, and behold it was *very good*.
And God rested on the seventh day.

No material creation. Introduction of the moral world. Age of man.

www.ingramcontent.com/pod-product-compliance
Lightning Source LLC
Chambersburg PA
CBHW032158160426
43197CB00008B/972